24 Gospel Favorites
Arranged for S.A.B. Choir
by Mosie Lister

Lillenas Publishing Co.
KANSAS CITY, MO. 64141

Contents

Wonderful Grace—Medley

H. L. and AVIS BURGESON

HALDOR LILLENAS
Arr. by Joseph Linn
Piano transcription by Lyndell Leatherman
SAB arrg't. by Mosie Lister

*NOTE: An orchestral accompaniment cassette is available for this arrangement (MU-2076C). Orchestration also available.

13
C
C°
C
C7
F
div.
Tak - ing a - way my bur - den, Set - ting my spir - it free;
17
F♯°
C/G
A♭7
C/G
G7
For the won - der - ful grace of Je - sus reach - es
C
21
C
G7
mf
me.
Won - der-ful the match-less grace of Je - sus,
Won - der-ful the match-less grace of Je - sus,
f

25
C
G7/B
G7
f
Deep-er than the sea, the roll-ing sea. Won - der - ful
Deep-er than the might-y, roll-ing sea. High-er than the moun-tain,
C
D6
D
G
grace, all suf - fi - cient for me, for e-ven me.
spark-ling like a foun-tain, all suf-fi-cient grace for e-ven me.
29
C
G
C
C7
Broad-er than the scope of my trans-gres - sions, Great-er far than all my sin and

33
F
F♯o
C/G
C/B♭
F/A
Fm/A♭
shame. Oh, mag-ni-fy the pre-cious name of Je-sus; Praise
G7
C
Em/B
Am
A♭
G sus
Dm
G
Altos
mf
His name. It is
mf mel.
39
*"It Is Glory Just to Walk with Him" (Burgeson - Lillenas)
C
F/C
glo-ry just to walk with Him whose blood has ran-somed me; It is rap-ture for my soul each
mf

43
G
Add sopranos
C
F
C
F/A
Fm6/A♭
day. It is joy di - vine to feel Him near wher - e'er my path may be. Bless the
43
C/G
G7
C
47
C
Lord, it's glo - ry all the way.
It is glo - ry just to walk with
47
G7
C
Him. It is glo - ry just to walk with Him. He will

51
rit.
a tempo
guide my steps a - right, Through the vale and o'er the height. It is
54
glo - ry just to walk with Him.
Legato
60
*"My Wonderful Lord" (Lillenas)
mp
f
My___ won - der - ful Lord, my

64
Bb F C F
won - der-ful Lord, By an - gels and ser - aphs in
64
68
C Cm7 F F7
heav - en a - dored. I bow at Thy shrine, my
68
a tempo
Bb poco rit. Dbm/Eb 2nd time to Coda F/C C7
Sav - ior di - vine, My won - der-ful, won - der-ful
2nd time to Coda
poco rit.
a tempo

74
F
F sus
F
F sus
Unison (or solo)
mp
Lord.
I have
74
78
Rubato
F
F7
B♭
F
found a deep peace that I nev - er had known And a
mp
82
D9♭7
Gm
B♭/C
C7
joy the world could not af - ford
Since I
86
Cm7
F7
B♭
B♭m/G
yield - ed con - trol of my bod - y and soul To my

90

F/C C7 F accel. a tempo Bb/F Bb/C D.S. al Coda 

wonderful, wonderful Lord. My

mp

90

D.S. al Coda

CODA

F/C C7 F Cm7 F

wonderful, wonderful Lord.

CODA

cresc.

98

Bb A/Bb Bb rit. Bbm/Eb Bbm/G mp F/C C7

My wonderful, wonderful

98

f rit. mp

102
Tempo I
F
F/E
F/D
F/C
Dm7
F/C
G sus
G
C
Em/B
Am
Ab+
Lord.
mf
G sus
Dm
G
106
C/B
C/A
It is glo - ry just to walk with Him. It is
G7
110
G/D
rit.
C/E
glo - ry just to walk with Him. He will guide my steps a - right, Thro' the

113
a tempo
F
A7/E
D
G
Dm
G
G7
vale and o'er the height. It is glo - ry just to walk with
117
C
F
F♯o
C/G
C7/B♭
F/A
Fm6/A♭
f
Him. Oh, mag - ni - fy the pre - cious name of Je - sus!
C/G
G
C
Gm7
C
Gm7
C
N.C.
ff
Praise His name!

J. W. H.

Majesty

JACK W. HAYFORD
Arr. by Joseph Linn
SAB arrg't. by Mosie Lister

Martial ♩ = 108

mf

simile

4

7

10

15

mf G

C

Maj - es - ty, worship His maj - es - ty;

mf

15

NOTE: An orchestral accompaniment cassette is available for this arrangement (MU-2100C).

Am7
C/D
19
G
Bm/F♯
Em
Em7
A7
F
Un - to Je - sus be all glo - ry, pow - er, and praise.
D
C/D
D
23
G
Dm/F
G
Am7
G/B
Maj - es - ty, king - dom au -
C
G/B
Am
27
G/D
thor - i - ty Flow from His throne un - to His

D
G sus
G
31
Am
own, His an-thems raise. So ex - alt, lift up on
31
D
C/D
D
G
high the name of Je - sus. Mag - ni -
35
Am7
D
C/D
D/C
B
Em
Am9
D7
fy, come glo - ri - fy Christ Je - sus, the King.
35

39
G
Am7
G/B
C
G/B
Am
Maj - es - ty, worship His maj - es - ty;
39
43
G/D
D
D7
G
Je - sus who died, now glo - ri - fied, King of all kings.
43
f
47
Cm
F
E♭/F
F7
So ex - alt, lift up on high the name of
f
47
f

Bb F/Bb Bb (51) Cm Cm7

Je - sus. Mag - ni - fy, come glo - ri -

F Eb/F F/Eb D Gm Cm9 F7 (55) Bb Ab/Bb

fy Christ Je - sus, the King. Maj - es - ty,

Bb Eb/Bb Bb Eb Bb/D Bb/C Cm7 Dm7 Cm/Eb

wor - ship His maj - es - ty; Je - sus who

59
B♭/F
F
died,
now glo - ri - fied,
Driving
E♭/F
B♭/F
E♭/F
63
B♭
B♭/A♭
E♭/G
E♭m/G
King of all kings.
B♭/F
F7sus
E♭/F
F sus
F/B♭
B♭
ff
Wor - ship His maj - es - ty!
8va

I've Been Changed

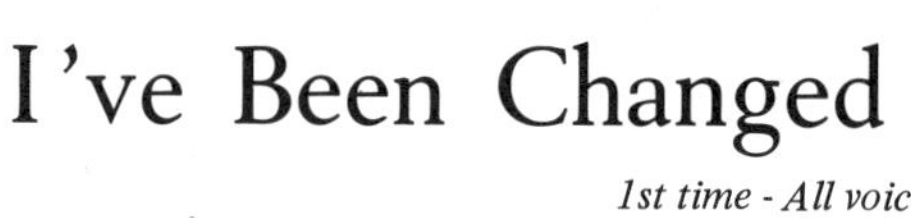

M. L. MOSIE LISTER

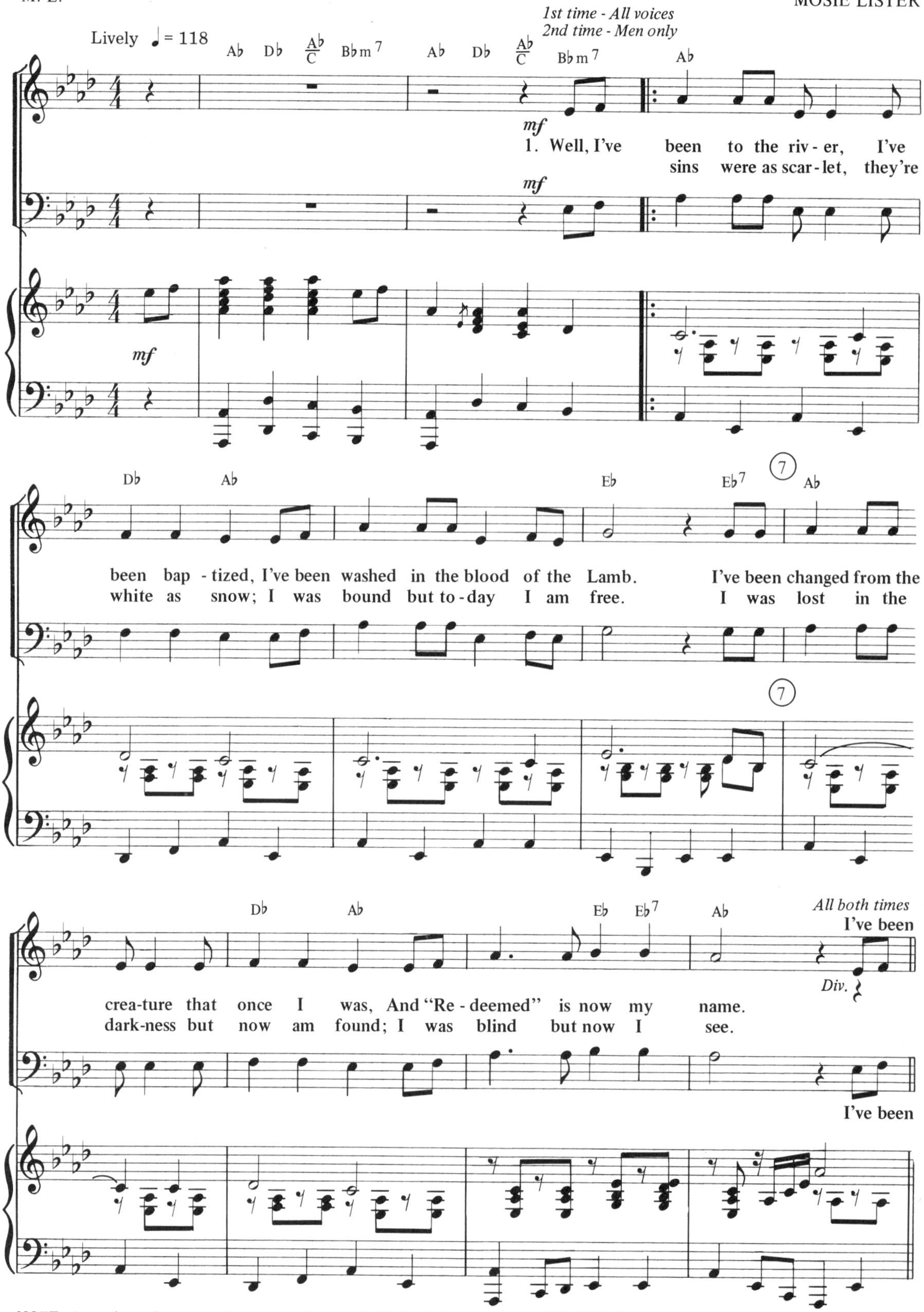
Lively ♩ = 118
1st time - All voices
2nd time - Men only
Ab Db Ab/C Bbm7 Ab Db Ab/C Bbm7 Ab
mf
1. Well, I've been to the riv - er, I've been bap - tized, I've been washed in the blood of the Lamb.
sins were as scar - let, they're white as snow; I was bound but to - day I am free.
Db Ab Eb Eb7 Ab
I've been changed from the crea-ture that once I was, And "Re - deemed" is now my name.
I was lost in the dark-ness but now am found; I was blind but now I see.
Db Ab Eb Eb7 Ab
All both times
I've been
Div.
I've been

NOTE: An orchestral accompaniment cassette is available for this arrangement (MU-1160C).

11
Ab Db Ab/C Bbm7 Ab Db Ab/C Bbm7 Ab Fm7 Bb7
changed, I've been new-born; All my life has been re - ar -
I've been changed, I'm new - born now; My life has been re - ar -
changed, I've been new-born; All my life has been re - ar -
11
Eb7 Bbm7 Eb7
15
Ab Ab7 Db Db7
ranged.
ranged. What a diff-'rence it made when the Lord came and stayed In my
ranged.
15
Ab/Eb Eb7
1 Ab
2 Ab E7
heart; oh, yes, I've been changed.
changed. 3. Like the
2. Though my
1
2

20
A
D
A
E7
poor He-brew chil-dren, I wan-dered long In a bare des-ert land to and fro.
24
A
D
A
E7
But I've crossed o-ver Jor-dan to Ca-naan's land, Where the milk and hon-ey
A
F7
28
B♭
E♭
B♭
flow.
When at last in His pres-ence I stand a-bove, He will
28 More energetic
f

F7
32
B♭
E♭
wipe all the tears from my eyes; And I'll thank Him for giv-ing a wretch like
32
B♭
F7
B♭
36
B♭ E♭ B♭/D Cm7
I've been changed, I've been
me Last-ing hope be-yond the skies.
I've been changed, I'm
I've been changed, I've been
36
B♭ E♭ B♭/D Cm7 B♭ C7 F Cm7 F7
40
B♭ B♭7
new-born; All my life has been re-ar-ranged.
new-born now; My life has been re-ar-ranged.
What a diff-'rence it made when the
new-born; All my life has been re-ar-ranged.
40

E♭
B♭/F
F7
B♭
44
Lord came and stayed In my heart; oh, yes, I've been changed. What a diff-'rence it
B♭7
E♭
B♭
47
F7
made when the Lord came and stayed In my heart; oh, yes, I've been
cresc.
B♭
B♭7
E♭
B♭
ff
changed. I'm changed!
(6)

'Till the Storm Passes By

M. L.
MOSIE LISTER
Arr. by Rick Powell
SAB arrg't. by M. L.

NOTE: An orchestral accompaniment cassette is available for this arrangement (MU-1149C).

Em7 Dm7 C
21
G
G7
C
3
'Til the storm pass-es o - ver, 'Til the thun-der sounds no
3
21
mp
Am7
25
D7 poco a poco cresc.
G
G7
f
more, 'Til the clouds roll for - ev -er from the sky; Hold me
f
25
poco a poco cresc.
29
C
C7
F
C/E
F
33
C/E
Am Am7/G
fast, let me stand in the hol-low of Thy hand; Keep me safe 'til the
29
33
f
mf

D9/F♯ G7 C F/G (37) C Am

storm pass-es by. When the long night has end-ed and the

(37)

mp legato

Ped. *

Dm7 C♯° Dm7 (41) G7 G9

storms come no more, Let me stand in Thy pres-ence on that

(41)

Dm7 G7 C F/G (45) C C7

bright, ___ peace-ful shore. In that land where the tem-pest nev-er

(45)

poco a poco cresc.

F
49
C/E
Am
Fm6/A♭
C/G
G7
C
comes, Lord, may I dwell with Thee when the storm pass-es by.
f
mf
dim.
53
G
G7
C
build gradually
Am7
'Til the storm pass-es o-ver, 'Til the thun-der sounds no more, 'Til the
mf
57
D7
G
B♭7
ff
clouds roll for-ev-er from the sky;
Hold me

61
Eb Eb7 Ab6 Ab Eb Ab
mf
fast, let me stand in the hol-low of Thy hand; Keep me
ff
mf
65
Eb Ab Eb Ab Eb F9/C
dim.
safe, keep me safe 'til the storm
dim.
Bb7sus Bb7
70
Ab
mp
rit.
Eb
(3)
pass-es, 'til the storm pass-es by.
mp
rit.

When the Roll Is Called Up Yonder

J. M. B.

JAMES M. BLACK
Arr. by Dick Bolks

NOTE: An orchestral accompaniment cassette is available for this arrangement (MU-2029C).

Db D° Ab/Eb Fm Ab/Eb Eb7 Ab
Ladies Div.
on the oth-er shore, And the roll is called up yon-der, I'll be there. When the
home beyond the skies, And the roll is called up yon-der, I'll be there.
3
15
Ab Ab6 AbM7 A° Bbm Gb/Bb
roll is called up yon - der, When the roll is called up
When the roll is called up yon - der, When the roll is
15
Brightly
Eb7 Bbm7 Eb7
19
Ebm7/Ab Ebm7 Ab7 Db Ab/C Bbm7 Dbm6/Fb
Unison
yon - der, When the roll is called up yon - der, When the
called up yon - der, When the roll is called up yon - der,
19

A♭/E♭
E♭7
1
A♭
D♭/E♭
2
A♭
roll is called up yon-der, I'll be there.
2. On that there.
1
2
24
rit.
Smoothly
Solo or duet
mp
3. Let us
Smoothly
rit.

30
Rubato ♩ = 92
AM7 A7 D A F♯m F♯m7 B7
la - bor for the Mas-ter from the dawn till set-ting sun; Let us talk of all His won-drous love and
Oo
Oo
mp
E9sus E7
ten.
A C♯7/G♯ F♯m A7/E D D♯o A/E
Brightly
a tempo
mf Unison
care.
Then when all of life is o - ver and our work on earth is done, And the
mf
Brightly
♩ = 120
mf a tempo
A/E E7 A Bm7/E A
38
A6
Div. f
roll is called up yon-der, I'll be there.
When the roll is called up
When the roll is
f

A M7 A♯o Bm G/B E Bm7 E7 Em7/A

yon - der, When the roll ___ is called up yon - der, When the roll ___

called up yon - der, When the roll is called up yon - der, When the

A7 D G9 (45) A/E Bm/E C♯m/E

___ is called up yon - der, ___ When the roll is called up

roll is called up yon - der, ___

(45) Strong

Dm/E N.C. A D6/A A

I'll be there

yon-der, I'll be there, ___ I'll be there. ___

cresc.

8va

ff

I Will Glory in the Cross

D. R.

DOTTIE RAMBO
Arr. by Joseph Linn
SAB arrgt. by Mosie Lister

NOTE: An orchestral accompaniment cassette is available for this arrangement (MU-1223C).

Fm/B♭
B♭ Cm
B♭7/D
18
E♭
B♭m7
E♭7
A♭
A♭M7
grace.
mf
grace, His grace. All glo - ry and praise shall rest up - on
mf
18
cresc.
mf
A♭m6
Unison
22
E♭/B♭
B♭sus
E♭
A♭ Gm7 Fm7 A♭/B♭
Div.
Him, So will - ing to die in my place. I will
22
26
E♭
A♭
3
E♭
glo - ry in the cross, in the cross, Lest His
3
26

30
A♭
Gm7
Fm7
E♭
A♭/B♭
34
E♭
mp
suf - f'ring all be in vain.
I will weep no
mp
30
34
mp
B♭m7/E♭
E♭7
2nd time to Coda
A♭
A♭m/F
A♭m6
38
E♭/B♭
B♭6
B♭7
more for the cross that He bore; I will glo - ry in the
2nd time to Coda
38
E♭
D♭/E♭
E♭
D♭/E♭
Unison
mf
cross.
My
mf
3
3

(44) Ab — Cb/Ab — Db/Ab — C/Ab — (48) Ab — Db/Ab

tro - phies and crowns, my robe stained with sin Was all that I

Melody

(44) March-like — 3 — (48)

Ab — *Div.* — Bb/Ab — Db/Eb — Eb — Db/Eb — Eb — Fm7 — Eb7/G — (53) Ab

Melody

feet, His feet,

had to lay at His feet, Un - wor - thy to

(53)

Gb/Ab — Ab7 — Db — Dbm6 — (57) Ab/Eb — Eb — Db/Eb — Eb7

eat from the ta - ble of life 'Til love made pro - vi - sion for

D.S. al Coda
CODA
Build to the end
62
A♭
A♭ Gm Fm7
A♭/B♭
A♭m/F
A♭m6
E♭/B♭
me. I will bore, I will glo - ry,
I will glo - ry,
glo - ry, glo - ry
66
F/B♭
G♭/E♭
F/E♭
f
in in the cross.
70
ff
E♭
8va

Come and See the Man
(at the Well)

M. L.

MOSIE LISTER

NOTE: An orchestral accompaniment cassette is available for this arrangement (MU-2093C).

17
G
G7
C
A7
He called it liv - ing wa - ter and He of - fered it to me,
He told me ev - 'ry - thing that I had ev - er done,
mf
Oo
17
21
D
D7
G
C/G
G
And I think that He must be the Man from Gal - i - lee.
And I think that He must be the heav'n-ly Fa-ther's Son.
He must be
21
Bm/D
Am/D
25
G
D7
come and see the Man at the well
Oh, come and see the Man at the well,
Oh, come and see the Man, come and see the Man
25

29
D7
Let Him give you wa - ter and you'll
G
C
at the well.
at the well.
you'll nev - er thirst a - gain.
29
C/G
G
33
G
Lis - ten ev - 'ry - bod - y,
C
A7
come and see the Man;
33
37
D
1 C/G
G
D.C.
Come and see the Man at the well.
37
1
D.C.

2
C/G
G
A7
43
D7
Oh,
come
and
see
the Man,
the
2
43
1,2
G
C
G
A7
3
G
C6/G
G
Man
at
the well.
Oh,
Man,
the
Man
at
the well.
1,2
3
49
49
8va
8va
8va

Come, Holy Spirit

13
F
C7/F
F
F7/A
Eb/G
F7
Div.
Come, Lord, as strength to my
Come, as a dew to my
Oh, let Thy sweet heal - ing
13
Bb
Bbm6
17
F/C
C7
weak - ness; Take me: soul, bod - y, and
dry - ness; Fill me with joy ev - er -
pow - er Touch me and make me
17
21
F
Db/F
1st time: go on
2nd time: D.S.
3rd time: go on
F
Bb/F
F
mind.
more. (to 3rd stanza) Come, Ho - ly Spir - it, I
whole.
1st time: go on
2nd time: D.S.
3rd time: go on
21

25
C7
Gm
Gm7
C7
need Thee;
Come, sweet Spir - it, I
25
F
29
F7
Eb/F
F7
pray.
Come in Thy strength and Thy
29
Bb
Bbm6
33
F/C
1
C7
pow - er;
Come in Thine own gen - tle
33
1

F
B♭/F
D.S.
2
C7
F
way. own gen - tle way.
F7/E♭
B♭/D
B♭m/D♭
F/C
mp
Oh,
Gm/C
C7sus
F
come, I pray.
slight rit.
pp

I Go to the Rock

D. R.

DOTTIE RAMBO
Arr. by Mosie Lister

NOTE: An orchestral accompaniment cassette is available for this arrangement (MU-1207C).

Bb/F F C Gm/F F
13
Bb Bo
lean on,
ref - uge,
no one wants to lis - ten? Who do I lean on, oh, yes, when there's
winds of sor - row threat - en? Is there a ref - uge, oh, yes, in the
13
F/C A/C# Dm F/A Gm Gm/D C7
17
no foun - da - tion sta - ble? I go to the Rock I know that's a - ble, I
time of trib - u - la - tion? When my soul needs con - so - la - tion I
17
F7 Bb/F F Gm
21
go to the Rock.
go to the Rock.
I go to the Rock of my sal -
21

C
A
Dm
B♭
B♭/F
F
C/E
25
Dm
Am
va - tion, Go to the Stone that the build-ers re-ject - ed, Run to the Moun-tain and the
25
B♭
B♭M7
G/B
G7/B
B♭/C
C7
29
F
Moun - tain stands by me.
The earth all a - round me is
29
C
F
Dm
A
A7
Dm
B♭
sink-ing sand; On Christ, the Sol - id Rock, I stand. When I need a

33
F D7 G9 C7 Bb/F
1
F A7 Dm
shel - ter, when I need a friend, I go to the Rock.
33
1
Bb Bb6/C
Unison
D.S.
2
F C7 Bb/F
Where do I
to the Rock.
D.S.
2
rit slightly
41
Deliberately—do not decresc.
F C Bb/F F
I go to the Rock.
41
Deliberately—do not decresc.

Jesus Paid It All

ELVINA M. HALL

JOHN T. GRAPE
Arr. by Dick Bolks
SAB arrg't. by Mosie Lister

NOTE: An orchestral accompaniment cassette is available for this arrangement (MU-1146C).

14
Choir both times
Je - sus paid it all; All to Him I
owe.
18
Sin had left a crim-son stain; He washed it white as
snow.
D.S.
Opt. solo 2. For snow, white as snow.
cresc.

27
F M7
F+
Gm/F
F M7
B♭M7
f
And when be-fore the throne I stand in Him com-plete, "Je-sus
27

31
Am
Dm
Gm7
F add6/C
C7
F
died my soul to save," My lips shall still re-peat, Will re-
re-peat.
31

Gm/F
36
F
Am/E
Dm
Am
D9♭
ff
mf
peat.
Je-sus paid it all; All to Him I
36

Gm C9♭ (40) FM7 Am F+/A B♭M7 E9 N/C

cresc. *f* *mp*

owe. ___ Sin had left a crim - son stain; ___ He

mp

(40)

f

(43) Am D9♭ Gm7 C9♭ Dm FM7/C Dm/B D♭/B♭ E♭9

washed ___ it white as snow. ___

(43)

mf

rall. (48) Gently Am D7/A Gm7 G♭M7 F

washed it white ___ as snow. ___

He washed

8va (48) Lightly

rall. *mp*

L.H.

The Happy Jubilee

RAYMOND BROWNING

ADGER M. PACE
Arr. by Otis Skillings
SAB arrg't. by Mosie Lister

(17)

B♭ B♭ D7

lee! ___ All the saints of all the a - ges in their

Ju - bi - lee! You will find me, for I'm watch - ing and my

(17)

(21)

E♭ B♭ E♭ Cm B♭/F F7

glo - ry will be there. Oh, I'm go - ing to that hap-py ju - bi -

lamp is trimmed and bright. Oh, I'm go - ing to that hap-py ju - bi -

(21)

B♭ REFRAIN (25) E♭ B♭

lee. ___ Ju - bi - lee! ___ Ju - bi - lee! ___

lee. ___ Ju - bi - lee! Ju - bi -

(25)

F7
29
B♭
Dm
Gm
C7
F
C7
lee! I am go - ing to that hap-py ju - bi - lee.
29
F7
B♭
33
E♭
B♭
Ju - bi - lee! Ju - bi-
Ju - bi - lee! Ju - bi - lee!
33
F7
37
B♭
Dm
Gm
F7
1 B♭ rit. E♭
lee! Yes, I'm go - ing to that hap-py ju - bi - lee.
Ju - bi-
37
1
rit.

B♭
(4+) a tempo
2
B♭
E♭
43
A♭
With that
lee!
Ju - bi - lee!
lee.
43
a tempo
E♭
47
B♭7
E♭
Gm
Ju - bi - lee!
I am go - ing to that
47
Cm
F7
Em7
B♭
B♭7
E♭
51
hap-py ju - bi - lee.
Ju - bi - lee!
51

Eb
55
Ab
Ju - bi - lee!
Yes, I'm go - ing
55
Fm7
Eb/Bb
Bb7
Eb
to that hap - py ju - bi - lee.
61
Ab
Eb
(6+)
Ju - bi - lee!
61

I Sing the Mighty Power of God

ISAAC WATTS

From *Gesangbuch der Herzogl,* 1784
Arr. by Otis Skillings
SAB arrg't. by Mosie Lister

NOTE: An orchestral accompaniment cassette is available for this arrangement (MU-2010C).

*Sopranos may sing to measure 32, or men unison

24
sing the good - ness of the Lord, that filled the earth with
8va
mp
food. He formed the crea - tures with His Word, and
28
(8va)
then pro - nounced them good. Lord, how Thy won - ders
32
(8va)

(8va)
are dis - played wher - e'er I turn my eye, If
36
I sur - vey the ground I tread or gaze up - on the
rit.
41
f
sky! There's not a plant or
Broad

flow'r be - low but makes Thy glo - ries known,
46
46
And clouds a - rise and tem - pests blow by or - der from Thy
throne;
50
50
While all that bor - rows life from Thee is

rit.
54
ev - er in Thy care,
And ev - 'ry - where that
rit.
rit.
58
man can be, Thou, God, art pres - ent there.
A -
rit.
men! A - men!
(7+)
rit.
8va

How Long Has It Been?

M. L.

MOSIE LISTER
Arr. by Rick Powell
SAB arrgt. by M. L.

*NOTE: An orchestral accompaniment cassette is available for this arrangement (MU-1131C).

17
Choir
D7
Em
Em7
How long since you prayed? How long since you stayed On your
How long since you knew that He'd an - swer you, And would
17
21
A9
A7
2nd time to Coda
Am7
D6/9
Ladies unison
knees 'til the light shone through? How
keep you the long night
21
2nd time to Coda
25
G
Go
G
Go
G7
B7
C
Co
long has it been since your mind felt at ease? How long since your
mp

C
Am/G
G
Choir
G7
mf
33
C
heart knew no bur - den?
Can you call Him your
33
mf
B7
Em
Em/D
A7/C♯
G/D
Friend? How long has it been
Since you knew that He
D13
D7
G
C/G
D.S. al Coda
Solo or unison
cared for you?
2. How
D.S. al Coda

CODA
Am7 Eb7 45 Ab G7 Ab Db/Ab Ab
through? How long has it been since you woke with the
Ab9 Db Dbo Db Db/Ab Ab Ab7
dawn And felt that the day is worth liv - ing? Can you
mf
53
Db C7 Fm Fm7/Eb Bb7/D
call Him your Friend? How long has it been Since you

Ab/Eb Eb13 Eb7 Ab Ab7 (61) Db

Solo or unison choir

knew that He cared for you?___ Can you call Him your

(61)

mp legato

C7 Fm Fm7/Eb Bb7/D Ab/Eb DbM7/Eb Eb9

ten.

Friend? How long has it been Since you knew that He cared for

Ab Ab7 Db Ab (7)

Choir rit.

you?___ How long, how long?___

rit. 8va

The Meeting in the Air—Medley

Arr. by Mosie Lister

NOTE: An orchestral accompaniment cassette is available for this arrangement (MU-2070C).

G7 (17)

Da - vid and his sling; You have heard the sto - ry

(17)

F/G G7 Dm7 (21) G7

told of dream - ing Jo - seph; And of Jo - nah and the

(21)

G9 G7 C G7 (25) C

whale you of - ten sing. There are man - y, man - y

(25)

CM7
C6
C
29
others in the Bible;
I should like to meet them
29
C7
F
33
all, I do declare.
By and by the Lord will
33
G/F
F/C
C
surely let me meet them
Melody
At the

37
C/G F/G Em/G G7 C G7
Melody
meet - ing in the air. There is
41
C CM7 C6 C
go - ing to be a meet - ing in the air, In the
45
G7
sweet, sweet by and by. I am

49
Dm7
G7
go - ing to meet you, meet you there In that
49
53
C
land be - yond the sky. Such
53
57
CM7
C6
C
sing - ing you will hear, nev - er heard by mor - tal ear; 'Twill be
57

61
C7
F
glo - rious, I do de - clare; And
61
65
G/F
F
F/C
C
C7/B♭
A+
A7
God's own Son will be the lead - ing one At the
65
69
Dmsus Dm
C/G
G7
C
There is
meet - ing in the air. There is
69

73
C
*"Pentecostal Fire Is Falling" (George Bennard)
go - ing to be a meet - ing in the air, In the
When the Church of Je - sus tar - ries,
go - ing to be a meet - ing in the air, In the
73
77
sweet sweet by and
G7
by. I am
Pen - te - cos - tal fire will fall;
sweet sweet by and by. I am
77
81
go - ing to meet you, meet you there In that
Sin and wrong will be de - feat - ed,
go - ing to meet you, meet you there In that
81

85
G+
C
land be - yond the sky. Such
sin - ners on the Lord will call.
land be - yond the sky. Such
85
89
sing - ing, oh, such sing - ing 'Twill be
She will march to glo - rious vic - t'ry
sing - ing, oh, such sing - ing 'Twill be
89
93
C7
F
glo - rious, I do de - clare; And
O - ver ev - 'ry land and sea,
glo - rious, I do de - clare; And
93

97
F
C
C/B♭
A7
God's own Son will be the lead - ing one At the
Lift - ing high the blood - stained ban - ner;
God's own Son will be the lead - ing one At the
97
101
Dm
Em/G
G7
C
meet - ing in the air.
Ho - li - ness her mot - to be.
meet - ing in the air.
101
105
C
G7
Pen - te - cos - tal fire is fall - ing;
105

109
G9
G7
C
Praise the Lord, it fell on me.
109
113
C
F
F♯o
Pen - te - cos - tal fire is fall - ing;
113
117
C/G
G7
C
Broth - er, let it fall on thee.
117

A♭7
123
D♭
D♭M7
D♭6
f
Oh, there's going to be a
127
meet - ing in the air, In the sweet, sweet
131
by and by. And I hope to

E♭m7
A♭7
135
meet you, meet you there In that land be -
yond the sky. Such sing - ing you will
D♭
139
D♭M7
D♭6
hear, nev - er heard by mor - tal ear; 'Twill be

143
D♭7
G♭
glo - rious, I do de - clare; And
143
147
A♭/G♭
G♭
D♭
A♭m/C♭
B♭+
B♭7
God's own Son will be the lead - ing one At the
147
151
E♭m
A♭7
D♭
Broaden
meet - ing in the air. And
151
Broaden

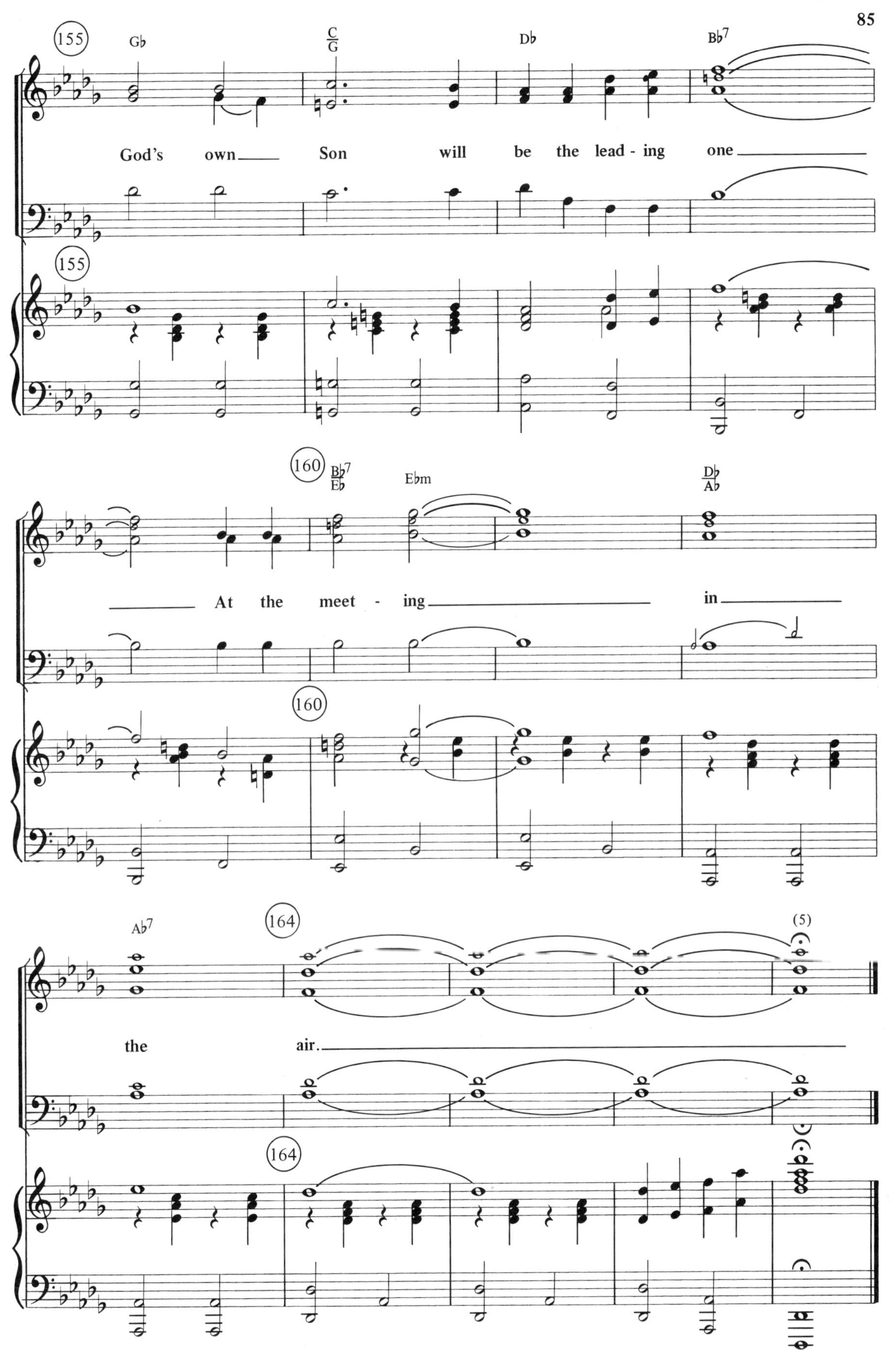
155
G♭
C/G
D♭
B♭7
God's own Son will be the leading one
155
160
B♭7/E♭
E♭m
D♭/A♭
At the meeting in
160
A♭7
164
(5)
the air.
164

The Lord Is In This Place

M. L.

MOSIE LISTER

Expressively ♩= 66

Db Eb7 Ab Bbm/Db A°/C Bbm Db6

p

Sure - ly, sure - ly the Lord ___ him -

legato *mp* *p*

Ab/Eb Eb7 Ab Db/Ab Ab 8 Ab

self is in this place. ___ Je -

mp *p*

Bbm/Db A°/C Bbm Db6 Ab/Eb Eb7

sus, Je - sus, Je - sus is here with love and

14
Ab
Db/Ab
Eb7
Bbm7
grace.
Pray, broth - ers, pray;
mp
3
18
Db
C7/G
Fm
Bb7
Pray, sis - ters, pray;
Pray till the moun - tains
a little stronger
22
Bb6
Eb
cresc.
Ab/Eb
mf
melt a - way.
For Je - sus is

26
Gentler
Fm
Bbm/Db
A°/C
near you and Je - sus will hear you; For sure -
Bbm
Db6
Ab/Eb
Eb7
Ab
Db/Ab
ly the Lord is in this place. Oh,
dim.
30
sure - ly the Lord is in this place.
pp
p
mp
R.H.

If You Believe

M. L.

MOSIE LISTER

E♭7
A♭
God was on their side; That jail-house door swung o-pen wide.
If you be-
13
D♭
A♭
B♭7
lieve, you shall re-ceive. There's not a trou-ble or care the
If you be-lieve, you shall re-ceive. There's not a
13
E♭
17
A♭
good Lord can't re-lieve.
care the good Lord can't re-lieve.
He is just the same to-day,
17

Bb7
Eb
Eb7
Ab
you on-ly need to pray_And be - lieve, you must be - lieve.
When Dan-iel
mf
21
Ab
Eb7
mp
Oo
sat with-in the hun-gry li-on's den, No-bod-y
Oo
thought
mf
that there was an - y hope for him. But all night
25
Ab
Ab
Ah
long the li - ons

E♭7
A♭
F
F7
Ah
mf
When Da-vid
nev-er took a bite; God took a-way their ap-pe - tite.
29
B♭
F7
stood be-fore the gi-ant with his sling, Go-li-ath laughed at such a
When Da-vid stood
Go-li-ath laughed
mf
29
mf
B♭
33
B♭
F7
pu-ny lit-tle thing. But Da-vid knew his faith in God would stand the test. He flung the
But Da-vid knew
33

37
B♭
E♭
rock— God did the rest. If you be - lieve, you shall re-
He flung the rock— If you be-lieve,
37
B♭
C7
F7
ceive. There's not a trou-ble or care the good Lord can't re - lieve.
you shall re-ceive. There's not a care the good Lord can't re -
41
B♭
C7
lieve. He is just the same to-day, you on - ly need to pray And be -
41

F7
Bb
45
F7
lieve, you must be - lieve;
Be - lieve, you must be-
45
Bb
F
cresc.
Bb/F
F7
f
lieve. Have faith in the Lord and be -
f
cresc.
f
49
Bb
Eb
ff
Bb
Growing
lieve. Be - lieve.
ff
49
(4+)
Growing
ff

Holy Savior

M. L. MOSIE LISTER

NOTE: An orchestral accompaniment cassette is available for this arrangement MU-2078C).

7
E♭
E°
B♭/F
Gm
C7
ho - ly name of Him___ who came, Re - stor - ing us to the
Lord of lords, Em - man - u - el, ___ God him - self___ is
7
F sus
F
11
Parts both times
B♭
mf
E♭
B♭
Fa - ther.
with us.
Ho - ly Sav - ior,
mf
11
mf
F
F7
B♭
15
E♭
Lord, we___ a - dore You.
Ho - ly
15

Bb
F
1
Bb
D.C.
2
Bb
Sav - ior, Je - sus, Son of God.
God.
1
D.C.
2
20
Bb
Eb/Bb
Bb
F7
Bb
mp
Oo
Oo
mp
20
mp
24
Eb
Bb
F
F7
rit.
Db
Ho - ly Sav - ior, Je - sus, Son of God.
24
rit.

Sing Hallelujah

J. H.

JACK HAYFORD
Arr. by Paul Johnson
SAB arrg't. by Mosie Lister

NOTE: An orchestral accompaniment cassette is available for this arrangement (MU-2005C).

13
D
F♯m
D7
G
G/A
Stand on His Word, se - cure, un - changed for -
Stands Christ, our King, His "peace be still" com -
D
D/F♯
17
G
G♯o
D/A
Bm
ev - er; And sing hal - le - lu - jah!
mand - ing; And now, hal - le - lu - jah!
Em
F♯m
G
G/A
21
D
G/D D
Faith - ful God, our Fa - ther.
I have peace un - end - ing.
C/A
C6/A
1
D
G/D D
C/A
C6/A

2
E♭
A♭/E♭ E♭
D♭/B♭
27
E♭
Gm
f
With haunt-ing doubt
E♭7
A♭
A♭/B♭
E♭
E♭/G
31
A♭
B♭/D
or pas-sion of temp-ta-tion, Sa-tan would
E♭
B♭/D
Cm
E♭7/B♭
Fm/A♭
Cm/A♭
Fm/A♭
Cm/A
B♭sus
B♭7
sift you and would seek to steal your joy.

35
Eb
Gm
Eb7
Ab
Eb/G
Ab
Bb
Hear Je - sus speak, "I've prayed for you— you'll—
35
Cm
Eb/Bb
39
Cm/Ab
Bb/D
Ab/F#
Gm
Cm
fail not"; And sing hal - le - lu - jah! I am
Ah And
39
Fm7
Gm
Ab6
Ab/Bb
Eb
D7
44
E
Solo (or choir unison)
f
o - ver - com - ing. When in the
44
f

G♯m E7 A E E/G♯ 48 A
fi - 'ry fur - nace of af - flic - tion Hell's
B/D♯ E B/D♯ C♯m E7/B A C♯m/A♯ B sus B7
pow'r would cast you, or some weak - ness lay you low,
52 E G♯m C♯m F♯m A/B B° C♯m E7/B All f
Stand on His Word, "I am the Lord, your Heal - er," And
Div. A B/D♯ A/G G♯m C♯m F♯m G♯m A6 A/B
sing hal - le - lu - jah! By His stripes He heals
sing

61
Stronger
E C C7 F Dm Am F B♭ B♭/C
me. Chil - dren of light, the dark-ness fast is
65
F F/A B♭ C/E F C/E Dm F7/C B♭ G7/B
gath - 'ring; Earth's black-est mid-night comes, its last tra - vail be -
69
B♭/C C F Am Dm7 B♭ B♭M9 B♭/C C
gins. Stand in the light— God's Word out-shines the

73
Dm
F7/C
B♭M7
C/E
B♭/G♯
Am
Dm
B♭M7
B°
F/C
shad - ows; And sing hal - le - lu - jah! Sing hal - le - lu -
73
77
F/A
Dm/B
C/E
B♭/G♯
Am7
Dm
C/D
D9♭
Build
Gm7
F/A
B♭6
B♭/C
jah! Sing hal - le - lu - jah! We've a bright to - mor - row.
77
Build
81
B♭/F
C/F
F
ff
Sing hal - le - lu - jah!
ff
81
ff
no rit.

Ceaseless Praise

FRANCES R. HAVERGAL

TOM FETTKE
SAB arrg't. by Mosie Lister

1
A♭/B♭
B♭7
E♭/G
A♭
A♭/B♭
B♭7
im - pulse of Thy love.
1
mf
2
A♭/B♭
B♭7
A♭/B♭
B♭7
E♭
16
A♭
f
B♭7/A♭
on - ly, for my King.
Lord, I give my life to Thee;
f
2
16
f
E♭/G
Cm
20
Fm
Thine for - ev - er-more to be.
Lord, I give my - self to
20

2nd time to Coda
B♭
G7/B
Cm
rit.
Fm
B♭7
E♭
Thee, Thine for - ev - er - more to be.
2nd time to Coda
rit.
25
Freely
E♭
A♭
B♭7/A♭
E♭/G
Cm
Cm/B♭
F7/A
A♭/B♭
B♭7
mp
accel.
29
a tempo
Flowing
E♭
C7/E
Fm
B♭7
1. Take my sil - ver and my gold; Not a mite would I with-
2. Take my will and make it Thine; It shall no lon - ger be
29
mp–mf

33
Eb
Bb/D
Cm
Cm/Bb
F/A
1
Ab/Bb
Bb
Bb7
hold. Take my mo-ments and my days; Let them flow in cease-less
mine. Take my heart; it is Thine own. It shall
Ab
2
D.S. al Coda
mf
praise.
be Thy roy - al throne.
CODA
Intense
p
Eb7
Abadd9
rit.
Abm6
be. Thine for - ev - er - more to be.

The Day of Miracles

M. L. MOSIE LISTER

Very smoothly

Bb Dm7/A Dm7/F Eb Bb/D Fsus/C F sus F7 (5) Bb

mf

1. God lives to -
2. Dark days may

f rit. mf a tempo

Gm Cm7 F sus F7 (9) Bb Dm7

day, though some would de - ny Him; His pow'r is real, though
come and trou - bles may shake me. Why should I fear? He

Eb Gm/D D D7 (13) Gm Dm Cm/G Cm

some would de - fy Him. A - ges have passed and He has not
will not for - sake me. Lost in the won - der of love so

rit. a tempo

NOTE: An orchestral accompaniment cassette is available for this arrangement (MU-1120C).

A♭7
17
B♭/F
C7
F7sus
F7
changed, And He al - ways will be the same. Some
true, I never could doubt it, could you?
21
B♭
Gm
Cm7
F sus
F7
25
B♭
folks say that mir-a-cles are not for to - day; They say that it's old-
They say
Dm
Cm7
F7sus
F7
29
B♭
Gm
fash - ioned to trust and to pray; But I be-lieve that mir-a-cles still

33
Cm Ab7 Bb/F C7 F sus
hap-pen to - day For those who pray and be - lieve.
F7 37 Bb Gm Cm F7
say to that moun - tain
mp mf
If you say to that moun - tain, "Be cast in the sea," Have
41 Bb Dm Cm F7 45 Bb
f
faith that nev-er fal - ters and so shall it be. The One who moves that
have faith that

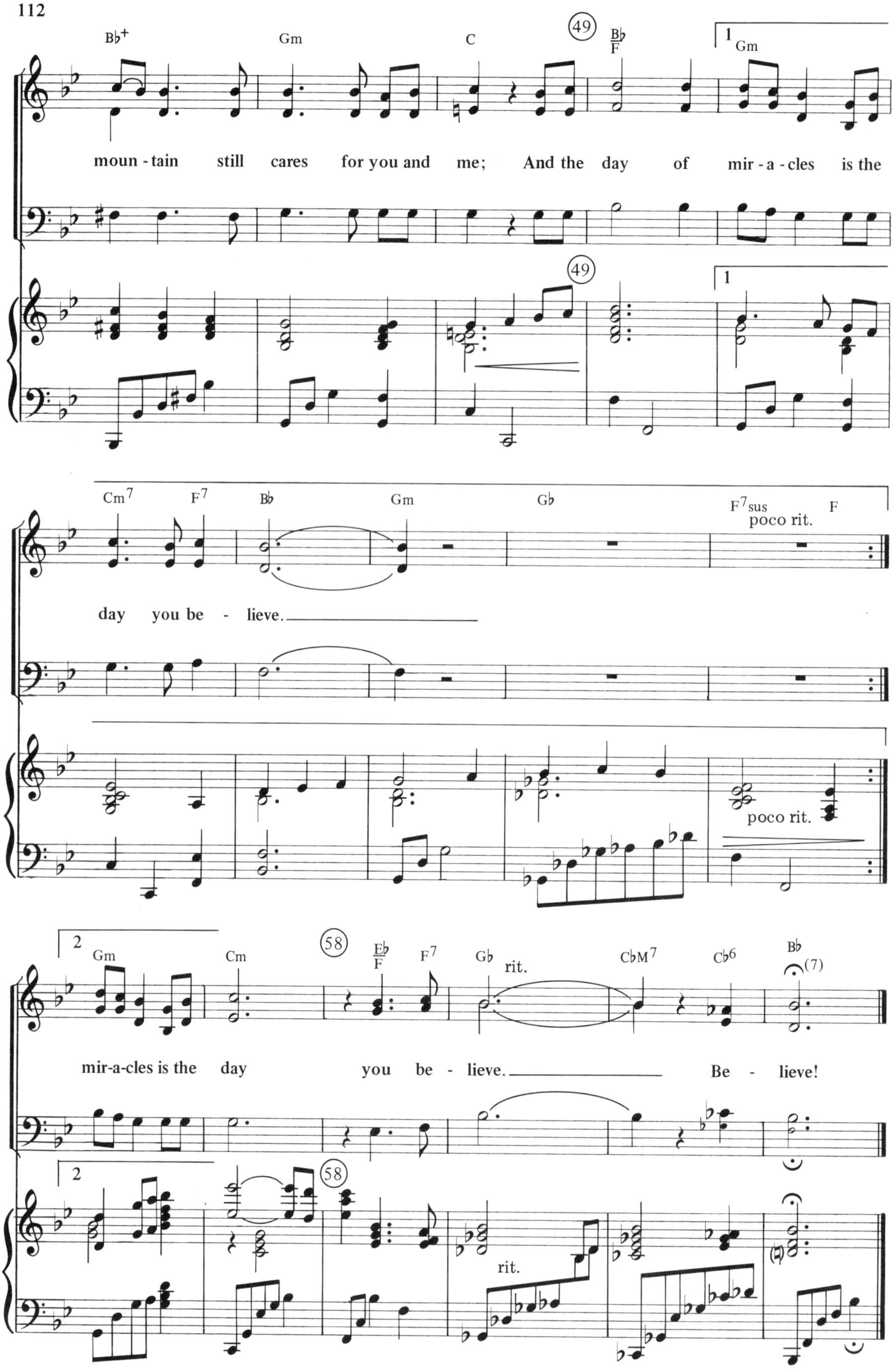
B♭+ Gm C 49 B♭/F 1 Gm
mountain still cares for you and me; And the day of mir-a-cles is the
Cm7 F7 B♭ Gm G♭ F7sus poco rit. F
day you be - lieve.
poco rit.
2 Gm Cm 58 E♭/F F7 G♭ rit. C♭M7 C♭6 B♭ (7)
mir-a-cles is the day you be - lieve. Be - lieve!
rit.

O Holy Night

A. A.

ADOLPHE ADAM
Arr. by Tom Fettke
SAB arrg't. by Mosie Lister

Dm/A
A7
Dm
12
F
peared and the soul felt its worth. The thrill of
name all op-pres - sion shall cease. Sweet hymns of
Bb
F7
hope, the wea - ry world re-joic - es, For yon - der breaks a
joy in grate - ful cho - rus raise we; Let all with - in us
16
Bb
Bb/A
Gm
Dm
All f
new and glo - rious morn. (1.) Fall on your knees; O
praise His ho - ly name. (2,3.) Christ is the Lord; O
f
16
f

20
Cm
Gm
B♭/F
hear the angel voic - es! O night
praise His name for - ev - er! His pow'r
F7/E♭
B♭/D
E♭
B♭/F
F7
di - vine! O night when Christ was
and glo - ry ev - er-more pro-
24
B♭
F
F7/E♭
1
B♭/D
E♭
born! O night, O ho - ly
claim! His pow'r and

B♭/F
F7
B♭
D.S.
night, O night di - vine.
D.S.
2
B♭/D
E♭
B♭/F
F7
B♭
glo - ry ev - er - more pro - claim.
2
3
B♭/D
E♭
B♭/F
F7
B♭
slight rit.
glo - ry ev - er - more pro - claim.
3
slight rit.